Catchments

Catchments
Copyright 2020, E. A. Lechleitner

No part of this book may be reproduced by any means known at this time or derived henceforth without written permission of the publisher or author. The exception would be in the case of brief quotations embodied in the critical articles or reviews and pages where permission is specifically granted by the publisher or author.

Books may be purchased in quantity and/or special sales by contacting the publisher. All inquiries related to such matters should be addressed to:

Middle Creek Publishing & Audio
9167 Pueblo Mountain Park Road
Beulah, CO 81023
editor@middlecreekpublishing.com
(719) 369-9050

First Paperback Edition, 2020
ISBN: 978-1-7348208-0-5

Printed in the United States

Cover Design: David Anthony Martin
Author photo: Monte Stevens

Catchments

E. A. Lechleitner

Catchments

Seasons of Snow……………………………………………..8
Island……………………………………………………….9
Catching……………………………………………………10
On the Saint Simeon Farm Road with Monet, 1864…………...11
Son…………………………………………………………12
The Year of the Grizzly…………………………………......13
Training Wheels……………………………………………14
Two Passages………………………………………………16
Your Voice………………………………………......………17
Solstice Questions…………………………………………..18
I Need Only These Five Things……………………………..19
Till You Do Death Part…………………………………......20
Split……………………………………………………….......21
Scattering…………………………………………………......23
The Law of Grief …………………………………………...24
Falconry……………………………………………….........25
After a Painting by Marc Chagall……………………...……..27
Anabasis………………………………………......………….28
You Are My Child………………………......……………….29
Below……………………………………………......……...30
Root……………………………………………......………..31

Seasons of Snow

Autumn
shakes the branches
free of leaves
to step naked into

Winter
bark grows blacker
competing with night
until each swallow each

Spring
window full of blossoms
and snow the size of

Summer
branches bow
to a late white ovation
placing in my reach the top fruit
so sweet

the splitting wood.

Island

In anatomy, a cluster of cells separated from surrounding tissue.

When you descended from my body,
there was a moment your head crested
between contractions
and the doctor said
        Wait.

A moment when the room turned away
from me
and I was set adrift from the continent of family.
In those few seconds, I knew
what I had suspected
since I left my own mother's womb:
that we are alone and surrounded by water
without so much as a palm tree.

And yet,
there *you* were,
stuck in my vaginal craw
and that is when I knew
I would slay anything that rose up against you,

that I had rejoined the land that calved me.

Catching

Through the summer screen,
the name by which I am known to only one boy in all the world,
begs.

Circling the house,
called on by his desperate note,
I find him leaning into shingles,
legs dangling from the garage roof

hopelessly far from landing, terribly near.

Do I run from sight to bring a ladder
or stay until he drops--
onto my hard bones,
poor pillows for his falling?

Long after he is safely down
and grown and gone

still
I ask this question.

On the Saint Simeon Farm Road with Monet, 1864
 --after Rilke

We go on looking

at the wrong things.
The light,
not the darkness light deepens.
The horizon,
not the breeze.
The thrusting branches,
not the knuckles pushing through.

We keep on asking

the wrong questions.
We ought to wonder
whether this road is open
       before us
or beneath,
to draw us
       on
or in.

Clouds keep throwing shadows down
before us

still, we go on

looking.

Son

Just past the police department
she sees him, one with dirt bike,
toss a wrapper
with no more notice than a smoker
flicking ash.

Surprised to find it Snickers,
not cigarettes,
she follows him,
wondering,
if it really does take a village,
should she catch up,
berate him,
remind him that he will inherit
what he so carelessly fouls?

But the cut of his hair holds her back,
his lanky familiarity,
the complexion of his exposed arms--
so like her own.

As he glances over his shoulder
to see who's stalking,
his young cheek
brings her back:
her son, no more 14,
taller,
grown and far away.

Still, she wonders,
passing him as he slows down to get her off his back,
what if time had turned
and given her another chance?

She doubles back, pulls alongside
and retrieves the shiny silver
paper.

The Year of the Grizzly

A young park ranger in Glacier,
you carried a pistol,
in self-defense, of course, and in defense of others.
Two young women had been mauled to death that summer,
after all.

A wife, two children and three states later,
after you used that same pistol in self-offense,

I dreamed you walking through the front door:

mustard yellow hunting coat, red flannel lining,
its pockets almost big enough
for the small child I once had been.
The black Labrador on your heels,
lapping at the game bag
and banging her long black tail against door.
Everyone so glad to see you.

Not me.

I stood down the long hallway,
outside my bedroom,
arms folded across my budding chest,
because you unlocked
your temple
using that key forged to protect,

and left me on the other side of the door,
wanting you to carry me down the hall
piggyback to bed,

once more.

Training Wheels

I.
I need your help threading the brittle film.
I want you to sit down and watch the movies of that summer with me.
The jerky soundless images of you in dress shoes and tie,
sleeves unbuttoned and rolled up to your elbows,
running behind the bike, newly stripped of its training wheels.
I want you there when the screen reveals what I could not see
as I balanced perfectly:
you let go.

II.
You had to take the key from its hiding place
and unlock the drawer beneath the rifles.
You had to open the box
and lift the cold weight like a dead thing in your hand.
You had to put the gray slug inside.
And hook your finger.
You had to know.

III.
I need your help threading the brittle film.
       You had to take the key from its hiding place
       and unlock the drawer beneath the rifles.

I want you to sit down and watch the movies of that summer with me.
       You had to open the box
       and lift its cold weight like a dead thing in your hand.

The jerky soundless images of you in dress shoes and tie.
       You had to put the gray slug inside.

Sleeves unbuttoned and rolled up to your elbows.
       You had to hook your finger.

Running behind the bike, newly stripped of its training wheels.
                You had to know.

I want you there
when the screen reveals what I could not see
as I balanced perfectly:
                You let go.

Two Passages

You placed me in the warm soft tissue
of your longing for life
where I grew your dreams
to bone, muscle, heart.
With your right hand you brought me through,
but with your left you made another passage,
back to the dark mother.
They could separate me
from the body I grew inside
but had no clamp to stop the father blood
that fed me even as it washed
the sheets where I was made.
And so I wander between an inheritance of violence and of love
trying to learn something about happiness
that is just out of reach.

Well now you sleep,
now you sleep.
Let me go to do your dreams.

Your Voice

In the picture on my dresser,
you are standing by a picnic table
tuning the radio,
trying to find the news or the homecoming game
or Marty Robbins singing "Cool Clear Water."
But the radio is in the dark bottom,
your expression is the fulcrum:
> head cocked, eyes up and to the right, lips pursed,
> nostrils taking in air,
> even your skin listening
> as if for something far away.

I hold the picture to my chest hoping to hear what called you away.

Stumbling on a recording of you
was like finding a bone from your wrist in the tackle box.
Worried about stirring your rest,
it was weeks before I could thread the cellophane across the heads
and press Play.
Then,
the flood of your voice:
> too fast, too high,
> details drowned out by the freight train passing
> one block away.
> You on one side, I on the other.

In the coast guard,
your voice was the lifeline for a ship full of fathers and sons.
If I had a radio and you whispered into the top of a funnel cloud,
could I hear all the things I need to know that you took with you?

Or at least the timbre of your voice
when you tucked me into bed
and announced my name to sleep.

Solstice Questions

I. North
Outside, ice climbs your tree and splits it open
like porcelain slammed down in pain.

As children, we gave our Santa letters to the fireplace
because he could read smoke, you said.

When we cremated you
did God peer out his window
at a moon gone red with ash?

II. South
No taller than the rim of your hip waders,
I ran to keep pace with your stride,
sat on the shore beyond reach of your hook,
piling rocks, carving sticks.

Now, I walk to remember.

The arc of your wrist
whipping line out and out and out some more
till the fly would land right where you saw the Browns rise.

If I spooned all the gravel from this river
would I find you there?

I Need Only These Five Things

The dog to come when I call.
The floor to stay clean.
The window not to break
when I pound my fist against it.
My hand not to bleed.

The sky--
just as you left it.

Till You Do Death Part

In the corner of your closet,
sole against the wall:
one sensible red shoe.

Half-inch heel.
    Already you were taller than he
    and older.

Not much worn.
    14 years of short nights.
    31 years of unending days.

Size 11.
    You said it took so long to
    settle because it wasn't easy finding
    a man with the same size shoe.

Department store brand.
    You divided the expense of waders.
    One at a time on the water, calling the fish.
    One at a time anchored to shore,
    with a length of rope thought long enough.

Paid for with cash.
    One red shoe.

You would have no other.

Split

I. May Day
The black bark
grows blacker in the damp
as though competing
with descending night.

My window is full of
cherry blossoms
and snowflakes
the size of cherry blossoms
lit up with dusk.

II. Graft
He was five years dead
when spring snow,
like an axe,
split the cherry tree
you had planted that first year,
and split you as well.

With little salvage
you left the torn bark behind,
planted
another outside a new window
so you could grow old together.

III. Blossoms
Every year it grew straighter.
You, bent.
It was as tall as the house
when you emptied yourself
under its canopy.

In that spring's snow,
half its bare arms bent
as if reaching down to swaddle you
or brush the thin strands of hair from your emptied eyes,
until they snapped.

But the trunk held.
And the other branches propelled you
In a rocket of blossoms.

Scattering

A circle of thunderstorms hangs like theatre drapes
hiding the Rawahs to the east,
the Never Summers to the south,
the Zirkels, west,
the Snowies, north,
and hastens us in our rowing.
The sky will lend no time for prayer.

Startled by lightning
we hold the oars out.
Surprised how small the shore has grown,
how quickly,
we choose *this* place.

The white cardboard box wedged under my knees
gives up a plastic bag with the heavy gauge of Ziploc freezer storage.
I slip my left hand under as I would to lift a baby,
as you did me,
though you are half the weight.

I untwist the metal tie in its green paper sheath
as if I were about to make toast.

Careful to submerge the opening
so nothing of you blows back to us,
it is done.

Your ashes are like flecks of glass
the Browns and Rainbows swim through,
unaware.

Before you settle in the rich dark bottom

we are back,
back on shore
just as the first big drop splatters the powdery dirt
like a stone dropped on water.

The Law of Grief

I did not cry when your eyes turned from glazed to glass.
I did not cry when they dressed your body
nor when I braided your hair one last time
pulling it back from your face
beyond care then for the strays that fell across it.

When I sent the word "dead"
to your son, traveling by train between India and Nepal,
the writing finally made it real,
but I did not cry.

I did not cry at the mortuary, speaking your name,
nor at the service, hearing your stories.

I did not cry when sorting your shoes and letters and cooking pots
into cardboard boxes marked
Toss, Give, Recycle, Save.

I did not cry scattering your ashes with his
into Delaney Butte Lake
where you cast so many summers of your marriage.

When I walked into your room
and turned off the light beside your bed,
I did not cry.

Sitting on the floor,
almost a year to the day,
cradling your dog's blind head in my lap
while the vet shaved her hind leg to inject death,
which we could not do for you,
I wept.

Awake in the attic of your house
listening to the branches of your spruce
snap one by one under the weight of spring snow,
--hollow bones cracking under gravity and neglect--
into the pillows I emptied myself.

Falconry

My mother would be a falconer,
now
and I
the falcon.

At first she keeps me very close:
belled, jessed and blind
on her leathered hand.

We walk like this across the heath for hours.
Her soft feather, stroking,
she calls out secrets she had forgotten to shed
and some things she wants to repeat:
        my name, my name.

On the third day, still blind,
I take fresh kill from her open palm,
my head jerking as if attached with ratcheted gears.

Then
the reward for not drawing blood:
        the rufter comes off and I am sighted new.

Some time later she makes a long tether from her skin,
braiding it strong, as she always wore her hair.
This rope hangs, not down to the small of her back,
but across the large sky,
and I, on the tail of it, learn flight,
chasing a broken wing nailed to a board.

My mother would be a falconer
now.
And I
the falcon.

Some days a long-winged peregrine
sailing the open wheat fields
and taking quail mid air with one clean snap.

Other days the smaller accipiter,
perched on the 10th floor ledge
waiting for the drunk to loosen from the dumpster
a rat whose fat belly will be a handle
when I make him my purse.

But always I return to her gloved hand
because when I would be a falconer,
she will come for me.

After a Painting by Marc Chagall

She turns away from him,
sometimes,
towards dawn.
and settles back against the cup of his body
as though she were warm water waiting to be sipped.
His arm reaches along the length of hers, seeking
her softly-fisted hand to cap with his own
as if it were a newel post and he, descending a stair.

Thus nested, they will, sometimes,
rise up to the ceiling, through the attic, out the roof
and float over the town.

Dropping thoughts into chimneys,
freeing kites from the tangling fingers of trees,
cutting along the edge of properties
they know so well from the ground.
In the gray still life between the moon already gone and
the sun just promising the horizon,
they cast no shadow.

Later, past dawn, she wakes.
Sometimes
on the other side of him.
Cheeks still cool from dreaming,
she pulls pieces of cloud from his hair.

Anabasis

Swimming away from moorings
you discover me lolling in the swells,
a sleepy warning against deep keels.
Your surf-slicing hand at the small of my back,
we tread water as you unlearn the shore.

Then you climb into a white-washed skiff,
tipped into the distance.
Your shoulders in red long johns
hunch over nets alive with mica scales
I cannot see.

Soon, I will wake to you,
a small interruption on the horizon,
head turned toward me,
arm raised in salute.

You Are My Child

But I would not
take the soft cartilage of suffering
from your sockets,

not dry up your tear ducts
or float your pain
or fill the empty place
that dulls your eyes.

You are my child
and I would slip you my life shirt
to keep your chest from naked death
before mine.

But I would not give you the breath of forever.
Life you shine and spend
tarnish and spend
and spend.

I would only give you a pocket
to pull it from.

Below

On my narrow bed
arms folded against the cold,
muffled notes rustle me.

At first I think a power surge has kicked on the kitchen radio,
but then whole passages abruptly end,
begin again.
Measures repeat.
The tick, tick, tick of the metronome emerges
in the space of breaths too distant to hear.

The faint percussion
reminds me I was expecting you--
of course you would come.

The slamming of the screen door already out of range,
your arrival cannot stir me,

but your voice reaches deep.

Embraced,
I lean away from worry
into the thump, thump, thump
of your foot on the pedal

dull as blades of dirt
landing.

Root

It is Thanksgiving day and I
am digging, deep into the cold but still pliant earth
as, only a year ago, the surgeon dug deep in me.

Having declined invitations to gather at fat tables,
I choose to worship here
finally harvesting the last of the root vegetables:
carrot, beet, potato, parsnip, yam--
trying to know the difference between rutabagas and turnips

while the ground entreats.

Cupped hands empty where it yields these fruits,
pleading,
reluctant to lend me one more day,
impatient to take me in.

But not today.

Not today.

Acknowledgments

This collection would not be without the support of the Writing Lab: B.J., Doug, Felicia, Kathy, Nancy, Norma, Randy, Roger and especially Ronnie--for her leadership, encouragement and wisdom. Also a shout out to my parents, sibling, kids and grandkids—this is from and for you: the challenge, inspiration and love! And a special thanks to Pete—for the ongoing adventure.

About the Author

E. A. (Beth) Lechleitner has lived in Northern Colorado her entire life but has made a habit of traveling far from home whenever she can, even if only in her mind. She recalls writing her first poem as a pre-teen while riding past the Tetons in a white Chevrolet station wagon on a road trip with her mother, father and brother. Her career has been split between high tech marketing and education. She currently teaches writing at Colorado State University and owns Second Letter, an editing, writing and creativity coaching business. She irregularly muses about writing and promotes local writing events on her blog: Second Letter Writing Salon. She has two children and four grandchildren. Some of her poems have been included in the collection *Begin With Leaves* and the Pathways Hospice publication *Canceling the Milk*.

Middle Creek Publishing Titles

Fiction

Messiah Complex and Other Stories	Michael Olin-Hitt
Sphinx	Andrea DeJean
The Yellow Field	Peter Edward Burg

Poetry

Span	David Anthony Martin
Deepening the Map	David Anthony Martin
Phases	Erika Moss Gordon
Cirque & Sky	Kathleen Willard
Lessons from Fighting The Black Snake at Standing Rock	Nick Jaina
	Leslie Orihel
Wild Be	One Leaf
Bijoux	David Anthony Martin
Sawhorse	Tony Burfield
Almost Everything, Almost Nothing	KB Ballentine
Kimono Mountain	Mike Parker
p a l e o s	Hoag Holmgren
I	Bengt O Björklund
Across the Light	Bruce Owens
Faces of Fishing Creek	Kyle Laws
a daughter's aubade	Mara Adamitz Scrupe
Secondary Cicatrices	Lynne Goldsmith
Unraveling the Endless Sky	Sandra Noel
The Ground Nest	David Anthony Martin
A Wild Silence	John Noland
The Shaman Speaks	Joseph Murphy
Erodes On Air	Mark Goodwin
Hush	Rosemerry Wahtola Trommer
Catchments	E. A. Lechleitner

Non-Fiction

No Better Place: A New Zen Primer	Hoag Holmgren

About Middle Creek Publishing

MIDDLE CREEK PUBLISHING believes that responding to the world through art & literature — and sharing that response — is a vital part of being an artist.

MIDDLE CREEK PUBLISHING is a company seeking to make the world a better place through both the means and ends of publishing. We are publishers of quality literature in any genre from authors and artists, both seasoned and as-yet undervalued, with a great interest in works which may be considered to be, illuminate or embody any aspect of contemplative Human Ecology, defined as the relationship between humans and their natural, social, and built environments.

MIDDLE CREEK's particular interest in Human Ecology is meant to clarify an aspect of the quality in the works we will consider for publication, and is meant as a guide to those considering submitting work to us. Our interest is in publishing works illuminating the Human experience through words, story or other content that connects us to each other, our environment, our history and our potential deeply and more consciously.